T0294541

Other Books by Charles Bernstein

Disfrutes

Parsing

Poetic Justice

Shade

Senses of Responsibility

Legend (with Ron Silliman, Steve McCaffery, Bruce Andrews, and Ray DiPalma)

Controlling Interests

Charles Bernstein

ROOF

FOURTH PRINTING.

ISBN 0-937804-03-7
Library of Congress No. 2004090228

Some of these poems were originally published in *This, Rocky Ledge, Sun & Moon, Gnome Baker, Renegade, Mag City*, and *ROOF*. Acknowledgement also to the National Endowment for the Arts for a Creative Writing Fellowship for 1980.

Roof Books are distributed by
Small Press Distribution
1341 Seventh Street
Berkeley, CA. 94710-1403.
Phone orders: 800-869-7553
www.spdbooks.org

 This book was made possible, in part, with public funds from the New York State Council on the Arts, a state agency.

ROOF BOOKS
are published by
Segue Foundation
300 Bowery
New York, NY 10012
www.seguefoundation.com

CONTENTS

Controlling Interests

MATTERS OF POLICY

On a broad plain in a universe of
anterooms, making signals in the dark, you
fall down on your waistband &, carrying your
own plate, a last serving, set out for
another glimpse of a gaze. In a room
full of kids splintering like gas jets against
shadows of tropical taxis—he really had, I
should be sorry, I think this is the ("I
know I have complained" "I am quite well"
"quit nudging")—croissants
outshine absinthe as "la plus, plus sans
egal" though what *I* most care about
is another sip of my Pepsi-Cola. Miners
tell me about the day, like a pack of
cards, her girlfriend split for Toronto. By
the ocean, gripped in such an
embrace—these were blizzard
conditions & no time for gliding—
she promised to keep in touch. The ice
floes, at this point we had already floated
far past our original sightings, made for a
pretty picture but mostly nobody payed attention.
The next best thing, New York draft, my
own opinion, the National Express, no
doubt, no luck, next election, next
month.... Together, though not always in the

same degree, with a sense of their
unworthiness & admiration as to the number
that are wonderfully changed without any
motive, view, design, desire, or principle of
action. "How much is there, in particular,
in the things which have been observed."
"How lovely did these principles render him
a life." Next session, several occasions,
seems to say, thanking you for, so there will
be a, that is my—. At last the soup
is piping hot, the decks swashed, all appurtenances
brushed aside. Across the parking lot you
can still hear the desultory voices of the men
chatting about the dreary "affaires de la monde"
that they seem to find so interesting. You
take some white flowers out of the vase, the
one you postured that you no longer cared about
but which is as close to your heart as
that chair from which you wistfully stare
at the charming floral tableau, & bring
them into the kitchen where you fix yourself a
bowl of ice cream. It was as close as
that. With a heart chilling suddenness,
the ground itself vibrating rhythmically to
your various aversions, a man pushes a
wheelbarrow full of fruit around the curve
just out-of-view. Canned peas kept frozen

out of an intense confusion &, greatly moved
by such things, a kind of light without heat,
a head stored with notions & speculations,
with a cold & unaffected disposition, as on the
one hand there must sometimes be. "If the
great things of religion are rightly understood,
they *will* affect the heart." Still, what an absurd
figure a poor weak man makes who in
a thunder storm goes against the flashes of
lightning with sword in hand. "No vision of
loveliness could have touched me as deeply
as this sad sight." In the summer
blackouts crippled the city & in the winter
snowstorms: & yet the spirit of
the place—a certain *je ne sais quoi* that
lurks, like the miles of subway tunnels, electrical
conduits, & sewage ducts, far below the surface—
perseveres. Green leather chairs are easily
forgotten just as the bath water brings
only minor entertainment. But we have
higher hopes. Let me just for a minute
recount the present standings. There is
no more white chocolate & the
banks are on holiday in Jamaica. All
the cigarettes have already been lit &
the mountains climbed & the chills
gotten over. It is the end of the

3

line. Even nostalgia has been used up &
the moths have been busy making their way
through all your very favorite attire. True,
there are still some loose ends, last minute
details that will never really be completed,
but in the main there is nothing left to
do. All the guests have gone home & the
dishes are done. The telephone is off the
hook. It is written that the wisdom
of the wise will be destroyed &
the understanding of the prudent will be
brought to nothing. & so it becomes
time for a little recreation—like she can
certainly butter that popcorn. We live in a
time of great changes. Revolutions have
been made in the make-up of the most
everyday of vegetables. The sky itself is constantly
changing color. Electricity hyperventilates even the
most tired veins. Books strewn the streets.
Bicycles are stored beneath every other staircase.
The Metropolitan Opera fills up every night as the
great masses of the people thrill to Pavarotti,
Scotto, Plishka, & Caballe. The halls of the
museums are clogged with commerce. Metroliners
speed us here & there with a graciousness
only imagined in earlier times. Tempers are
not lost since the bosses no longer order about

their workers. Guacamole has replaced turkey as
the national dish of most favor. Planes, even,
are used to transport people at their will. Collisions
have been eliminated in new debugged systems. Ace
reporters no longer worry about deadlines but
sit around talking over Pelican Punch tea about
the underlying issues. Everybody drinks the best
Scotch & drives about the freeways in specially
constructed "no crash" recreational vehicles. It is
all a great relief. For instance, exhaling while
walking four to six steps, taking the time to feel
each step like the frenzied businessman waiting for a
call from Morocco. The colored lights reflect not the
state of the soul or its long dark night of
incommunicable exultation, but simply descending
steps on a long spiral, intercepting spherical
enjambments that—try & try—are impossible to notice.
Often at night, standing there, my brain
racing behind some fragment of a chimera, &
yet, & so on, could you really accept that, don't
make it any harder on yourself, let's
make a fresh start just you & me, come
on we can, &c. At last the relaxing change,
the sofa, Alexandria, Trujillo. You looked
into my eyes & I felt the deep exotic textures
of your otherworldliness. A tangle of thorns bearing
trees, extensive areas in Asia, Australia, South

America. Rye, oats, &c. The tall grass
prairie of the pampas of Madagascar, Paraguay
& the Green Chaco. Lobsters, oysters,
clams, crabs, tuna fisheries, shrimp. (1) The use
of easy & fair surfaces along the general paths
followed by the water flow. (2) At & near
the surface of the wave profile. (3) Proof
of good design. (4) Submerged
bulbs. I read somewhere that love of the
public good is the only passion that really
necessitates speaking to the public. Yet,
far from that—& distance was by now a
means of propulsion to theories of design—
everyone seemed to go about their business
in the same old way. Active roll resisting tanks
pummeling towering carriages, conveyor belts
incapacitated for several weeks with psychomimetic
complaints, origami paper oblivious to the needs
of nuclear families racked by cancer scares, diabetes
mellitus, & too many visits to Stuckey's Carriage Inn
in Savannah. Disorderly memoirs pockmark the
literary crabgrass & the small voice within hums
dim tunes overheard in the houses next door. "But,
whatever wrong you may think others have done,
maintain, with great diligence & watchfulness, a
meekness & sedateness of spirit." "If a life
against which it was impossible to level one reproach,

6

a life that followed your example, gives me right

to your respect, if any feeling still pleads for

me in your heart, as long as my guilt is still

not absolutely clear, please don't forsake me at

this terrible time." The marvel is always at the

wick's end & the static a make-believe music

of the rectangles. What stretches will also, & quicker

than you think, come apart, the separated pieces

thereafter forever irreconcilable, with the memory of

their former state no more than a brood along the

boulevard of a reconstructed city, the new

lights & new gaiety masking the utterly out-of-mind

presence of the ancient city's darker history.

Take broom in hand & sweep the chestnuts off

the boulevard, not so much as a diversion,

which has long ceased to mute the facts, but

as a pantomime of what, some other time, you

might have done. Yet, there was a life

without all this. "Certainly, there be that delight

in giddiness" & yet, for the most part, I've told

you time & time again, better haul out the shovels &

picks, board up the stained glass, acrylic

the calendar. There's plenty of time but

few with enough integrity or intensity to

fill it with half the measure we've

begun to crave. The birds are falling like

flies, one by one, out of the sky of the imagination,

sitting ducks for any Jon or Jonathan to
trip over on his way to college. Miles of
cable keeping us in constant touch, entangle
us in the delightful melodies of the new
age—lavender police cars that emit high pitched
whirrs, insisting that the sky writing above us
is the dining place for our servants. Beyond
this front is a fair court & in all the corners
of that court fair staircases cast into
turrets—quarters in which to graze at
equal distance from each other, surrounded
by stately galleries & fine cupolas. You take
the extra moment with exceptional cheer & together we
begin to shovel away the accumulated dust that blows
in our eyes & moistens our faces. Gratings, already
apparent after the long row, seem not so much
to enclose as to place. Pacing every which way
after already uncountable fortifications at
the snack bar, the water on boil, the various
"day" papers discarded, phonodiscs rolling down
meticulously laundered shafts, conduits
to another in a series of dissolving
snapshots, indices, day-liners. At last, the
cabin cruise is over & the captain gently
chides farewell to us with a luminous laugh.
Diving into the water, I grab my harmonica
& bang out some scales, all this time regaining

my bearing, retracing the directions. Before too
long it's time for a break. I stretch out
on the balsa wood finish & turn to the notices.
The surrounding buildings have a stillness
that is brought into ironic ridicule by the pounding
beats of the bongo drums emanating from the candy
store a few blocks away.

OFF SEASON

The numerous

                    psyche, the curtains

          glowing elegantly in the wind, the fromage all worn

               each day, hills more tiring than

     (the)

                         next mirror. A clasp

                              "which you have used so many

     times before", to erase that a

                    without in any sense an

          angry hearted

which at any other time might

                    demand to be, look at—

          might as well (any, seems)

          month passing without the *chauffage* that

                              quando, por favor, presto

               & taking several wraparounds out his pocket,

Or that chill inside that makes you want to HE
               SAYS RETURN THE SWANS begins

          around the fire with your feet bandaged, chat—

while the snow slowly turns into a monastic simper,

               the simplicities of a sudden

                              expire. Without

     notice everyone starts acting differently, loud

                    screeching sounds

                         shock, when you

          habits

        is abandoned

the light switch

           mark carefully

    else much is

      (tubular, don't let

replaces as cheeks, squares, domino patterns

            lights, surfaces

        or a continual grinding on the mirror, says
        "no, prego" & doesn't stop short at, meticulously
        pressing the lines between the apprehensions,
                                the

who at various times were compelled

          helpsperson

             regal, pompous,

      which is regarded at various times from
      different porticoes, which anyway might look
      different as the time changes, the leaves turn
      umber, the blooms fade. ...at least
      the consolation in the "simple fact" of the
      next sight, the water drained from its various
      receptacle. So you take the tram as
      far as—

           ingots, interstellar

As the Alaskan coolies gently fold up their

     sheets, the whiteness blowing radially

   against the crisp tones of the night's

          chill. Already

        thousands of Moroccans

            are crowding the corridors

      but

better not be bothered
with two circular bulbs on either side
clay which was sandblasted away,
revealing genuine articles of
previous moments
in step formations, comparable
(aerially encoded, resuscitate,
armlessly
is very radiantly
but here's, *here's*
stomach pump, metal detector
mirroring the precise manners his father
used or was fed up
"out the corridor"
as detection is tested,
musculature—
at very much times on the intake, a
gets, whichs
who sinks into (now
imitations of morality, an
evasions of space
color, line of mouth, overall aeration
who used to be out at
homes, planets
according to the practice of
sideswipe
now known under several international

12

A resplendent regression

possibly autoclave, Kleenex

                broken articulation of wrist

bend, branched

    which does not return

though you

      which "all the memory in the world"

carries along with it

      makes plain the

simple desire for ———

    or respite from

its, location

    which at this very moment

THE ITALIAN BORDER OF THE ALPS

I've spent the years since. Primarily rowing. I'll phone. Next week after the tube roses are installed. Vivid memories. People remain. I have occasionally. Shops, sorting out how to become useful. A prolonged bout. Interest in useful plants. Aside from, a couple of trips, I do what I must. This is a pleasure. Exactly two weeks but more like. When she spoke. Two years to me. Patiently listen. I'd come up & out with. Anguish. I'm very well, thank you, not at all, you'll take a bath. Thucydides or Livy just get up the. Fact, you've been gone, is already repainted. At this point, I intend to think in terms of, "interest", "hobbies". This has included three and one half months. I was struck by the sadness and hardness in her face. And make it soon, because Patsy and Mommy are very lonely for Daddy. Please, place the plums. Yes, now I remember. Not layers of time it was like it would happen again later. I noticed many of them had been donated. Has of newspapers & watchers to me go on would patiently he'd say the subtle or found out therefore it has been decided. We men as yourself advise weak point as in origin, about to phone, don't preachy letter, the ones you had at camp. Ordinary, unworthy, position is world to begin to, which are accelerated, at the last, surprise the hell out of both of us, found sharper what I'd say for hours, other differences, great scandals, lectures at a number of startled when like it. Is which it became most brilliant, ever since, at all for a day. I thought it all over for a while, of manifold to be patient, but as often to return, I seem to hear, which identity consists in prattle, for action, in the classic judgment of a good deal of whispers. Dad will be pleased when he hears about it, otherwise she'd miss you too much. Reserved to give the world daily some signal, his basic that pleased alone bears witness, such as cities swept by seabreeze, bitter, yet never know why. Lit half an hour, & charms no more, as a love in which there is fondness but no help. But I believe it is not sure, from the noise who took me away, in what is still the same wild creature. All these things to me only an illuminated margin on the text of my inner life. A line of people waiting to see the lion. The pale lady waiting patiently. & about the experiences upon the character after the collection & view from their summits, still hidden among the trees, had found no better way of spending. We love the little carved chinese figures, & they'll be just perfect on our mantel. Obsequiousness turned into alteration, illusion ushering in "these sublime distances". On the road back from the whirlpool we saw them. Stealing behind. Reduced to sit observing details, their dead parents in fields to fertilize, identity of that mood, unrefined as dread these proportions by which to appreciate it. The panorama. In the evening sail down the stream. The chief leads his people into the deep ravine. However, your stationery is now ready & will be sent to you at once. No place so completely. Thoroughfares. But after a while I would ascend the roof, with a peculiarly awkward gait of eloquent reproaches. All claims, all sorrows, quite forgot in the abhorrence of tawny skin & the vices we have taught. *It has not been tried.* But now I think we will meet again. While at our feet the voice of crystal bubbles charms us away. We don't like to remind a good customer like you. Greater popularity, good looks, security, praise, comfort, leisure. I want to thank you for the lovely time I had at your house. It was one of the best times I ever had. The pictures are so beautiful too. I wish I. I hope you will let Anita come and spend a week with us. I wish we had a pond like. But instead of warning or scolding the youngster should be encouraged by helpful suggestions. Everybody was disappointed. I am fine: please send cookies. Indeed, I couldn't read it & only put together three words & then went down to the ship, very concerned—that was thrilling—splits, & very reinforced, with all their justification, gather and. Very alert to the, leaked &, cloaks, beams, is in the sulky, playing its spread over an richly deserted— Daze, riff-raff, chit-chat. All my friends say I'm lucky to have such a nice aunt. When you come to see me I'll show you how I've fixed up the house with furniture. I make believe it's a real house. Typical, vital. First, the external qualities of bodies. Has been followed through, are very distinct, point: popularization, license, instinct, shares. Unfortunately, such an army of light is no more to be gathered. Many little beetles on the wooden bench. Thickened reins. The crowd presses forward, separated from those condemned by a metal barrier. We may now see what is properly meant by working class culture. The experience is that of individual persons. Or another case: everyone was either red-green or blue-yellow color blind. E.g., they speak English. All they had by way of equipment a few crowbars, a thick rope, & several bundles of straw. The existence of this emotion. Efficient, smoothly coordinated. Eyes acting up. Not smell: transparent. Again slogans rocking the hall. Longings lose glimmer. Don't get me wrong, I'm not a tough guy, just careful. Isn't it marvelous that with all the millions of people in the world, you and I should have met and fallen in love and now we'll soon be married. Or do you think it was all planned that way long ago? Get up, push way. Big as it is we'll take it to pieces. It's something to wear & it's something you've wanted. I'm not joking, and if I seem to talk in circles it just seems that way. It all ties together—everything. Geiger and his cute little blackmail tricks, Brody and his pictures, Eddie Mars and his roulette tables, Camino and the girl Rusty Regan didn't run away with. It all ties together. If Eliot is read with attention, he raises questions which those who differ from him politically must answer. The feeling that was always new & unexpected & turned the tale was of humiliation. Steamers. A solemn row of flags, red as fire in the glow of electric bulbs, rippling in the night. The interior of the house. Spacious. This place belonged to a rich peasant before liberation. It was given to us during land reform. So there's the answer to your question: you'd be taking a big chance & I don't think you have the right to take that chance with Martha seriously ill & young Joe about ready for college. That if I was going to be a fighter, I would have to train around people. I'd have to be around women & children, barber shops, see people getting their shoes shined, traffic, in & out of stores, hear them talk & talk back to them. Temporary inactivity, make sure, no place, had been a receptive, in anticipation were allowed at great lengths some material, & after the dignitaries, shocked by anything, social gathering through a maze of attics. I believe in change & I understand the impulse that makes you want to strike out against regimentation & find new interest & adventure in a business of your own. Insatiable booms, cheers. Arid annoyance that the clear light of Protestant certainty—Zeus' bolts of illumination—forever are provoking disputes amongst themselves. Not so much hypnotized, transfixed. In rows, handles, placed, departed. Ambivalence falling in on actual cones of charm. Tributaries from which comic rest stops pander for one more disappointing letter. That's just the way it. In our studious, the shape of, everybody grouped, along the shore, clammy, pleasure and an, at approaches attended to, towards. I like hard work and I don't care how

17

long my hours are. I have an inquisitive and analytical mind, make a good appearance and get along well with others. Gives way to. A reality continually demanded of, given up, renovated. Or else the hygenics of personal encounter are bowled over by autodidactic posturings in the name of space. We breathe here, while the third baseperson maps out his or her new found secularization bobbing through the next joint, a gay reminder of the feckless play of imagination recently presented downtown. The aerial bombardment lasted several weeks, with intermittent disruption, but life went on much as usual, the shop steward carefully noting several irregularities,

COMPANY LIFE

consummation of impossible sorrows

residues of the previous

marks

as the motion of a glance

scatters, as

misled, a kind of

autumnal (puff

quickly rushes

for, around

only asked

makes much of

induced memory

shouting to

amorous

double view

I've

meant to tell you

all, this

otherwise unrecognizable

encountered

with escalators confining the

levels, we

overhear overmuch

are, am

shattered crystal, blown

much as melts

        & trickles, *I* wish

      miniaturized in our desires

as cubicle follows cubicle

    next to an out-of-doors

even more interior

      (too plain

a pie, glysemic

    hope for sudden

changes, lifts

out or made for

      clips

pen & tie

  you wish...

SENTENCES MY FATHER USED

Casts across otherwise unavailable fields.
Makes plain. Ruffled. Is trying to
alleviate his false: invalidate. Yet all is
"to live out", by shut belief, the
various, simply succeeds which. Roofs that
retain irksomeness. Points at
slopes. Buzz over misuse of reflection
(tendon). Gets sweeps, entails complete
sympathy, mists. I realize slowly,
which blurting reminds, or how you, intricate
in its. This body, like a vapor, to
circumnavigate. Surprising details that
hide more than announce, shells codifiers to
anyway granules, leopards, folding chairs.
Tables at party which is no less the surprise
anyway in here fashion prizes. Straps,
everyday kind of stores. Ruminate around
in there—listens for mandatory disconsolation,
emit high pitched beeps. Not so inevitable as
roads which bear no signs. I guess eyeglasses,
motor cars piled up behind large—heap tall—pulleys,
regarding each other with mild affection, like
whose pushing these buttons, or a
walk in the park, by the lake, rivers discoursing
at length, which makes you much more
tired than thinking about it, the grass

taller than you imagined just before, rocks
nimbly rolling down sides of inclines. Or
how one day it became inevitable that
you would go back, hair blazing,
and start the walk down, careful to
look on both sides of the poplar lined street,
and with steady pace, don't even pretend to
recall, finally arrive. A large room in which
the people chat amiably—a hush that descends
even on leaves. "In a twinkle of an eye
it comes, the great secret which arrests
outer motion, which tranquilizes the spirit,
which equilibrates, which brings serenity
and poise, and illuminates the visage with
a steady, quiet flame that never dies." Shunning
these because of a more promising
hope of forgetfulness, I can
slip back in, see the wire coil making its steady
progress, peer at the looks flashed in my face. Best
leave that alone, & not make any noise either, lie by
the pool absorbed in its blue. "But we are not
equals; we are mostly inferior, vastly inferior, inferior
particularly to those who are contained, who
are simple in their ways, and unshakable in their
beliefs." Screens popping up every which way, embarking
us on our journey. Lessons learned, the pages
turned over. Crevices eaten away by misapplication,

subsistence, clamor. *It is our furniture that is lacking and our fortune that we are powerless.* Fortunate. The history of my suffering: useless and. "Like we would have it today." Silk hat. Which I never expressed at the time. My sister Pauline, my brother Harry. Was very well ah to me it was sad. That could have aggravated. That may have brought on. The impression I got is everybody. Or I should say well groomed. But in appearances. Apoplexy. Any chance of accumulating money for luxuries. Never even challenged, never thought—that was the atmosphere we found ourselves in, the atmosphere we wanted to continue in. Exchange Buffet. Which is very rare. Which I hear is not so apparent. Which blows you away. Like the GE is here. We don't fear this. It will quiet down. Now I was not a fighter & I would run away but they surrounded me & put eggs in my hat & squashed them & I came home crying & my mother said what are you crying for if you go to the barber shop you'd have an egg shampoo & here you got it for nothing. Muted, cantankerous, as the bus puffing past the next vacant question, jarring you to close it down a little more, handle the space with. "Now I'm going

23

to teach you how to sell goods." No rush or
push. We just conformed because of the
respect we had for each other. Sky scraped
by borders, telling you which way, I had
better advise, or otherwise looney
tunes appear in the hall &, glass in
hand, you debate the enclosures. A sultry
phenomenon—drained of all possibility to
put at ease, but heat soaked all the
same. Recursive to a fault. Lips eroded,
tableware carelessly placed as if the
haphazard could restore the imagination.
Instantly insincere. I told you
before: even current things: the
advancement of medicine, the new
chemicals that were coming up, the cures
that were starting to break through.
Patent leather shoes. In a gentle way. I
wasn't very, I didn't have a
very, my appearance wasn't one of, that
one could take, well I didn't make
the. Nothing stands out. Nice
type of people. Rather isolated. Pleasant.
I had the same dream constantly: swinging
from chandelier to chandelier. Crystal.
In a crowd of people. Just
local. In shame. Closeouts, remnants.

I don't remember too much. Gad
was on my back everyday.
I always figured: what I could lose.
Those were my values. To me they were
good values. I didn't want to
struggle. & I could live frugally. I didn't
want to get involved. I didn't care
for it. Necessity made the. Which
can't be helped. *Meeting us on our journey,*
taking us away. Hooks that slide past
without notice, only to find out too late
that all the time that transportation
was just outside the door. Sitting there.
I felt badly about it but never made a
protest for my rights. We never thought
of that. I kept in short pants: what
was given we ate. Nobody had
to tell me this. Everything went into
the business: being able to take advantage
of an opportunity, create an opportunity.
It was just a job I had to do.
We were separated all the time. No
rowdyism, no crazy hilarity. Impelled
sometimes beyond hands, that forces
otherwise in a manner of. Interesting
conclusions leaving you stripped of
subsistence, trimmed beyond recognition,

& all the time the tree lined roads—perfectly
spaced—mock the inner silence that voids all
things. To take a step—"I had to"—leading
without gap to a treasury of ambitions. "In
here" I am whole. Or goes over piles of
rocks—cowboy, pharaoh, bandit—stealing looks
across the street so often crossed but never
lingered in. With a sense of purpose divorced
from meaning. Strictly misrepresenting by it
this loom of enclosure, a path that opens onto
a field, lost on account of open space. Never
enough, randomly rewarded. I get way in, feel
the surface tight around the shape, breaks
through. A canvas of trumped up excuses, evading
the chain of connections. As so far bent
on expectation. "Don't stay in here, then."
Earned by driving mile over mile of eroded
insistence. The plane swoops down low over
the city, the gleaming lights
below waken the passengers to the possibilities
of the terrain, a comfortable distance above
& back into the clouds. A moisture that
retains hope, damp cellars of glass in which
large rectangular tubes carry passengers to
various levels, concavities really, endless
expanses of planes stacked on planes. Leaving
this place, so hugely exiled for whatever

bang of misprision you take the time out for,

a cacophany of shifts, tumbling

beside the manners you've already discarded,

falling among—in place of—them. The laugh

is worn out and you make your way amid

shocks and rebounds to the next counter,

allowing for the requisite number of "of course

you're right" "I never could have" "let's

try it again". Misled by the scent, you

spend the whole day trying to recover

what was in your pocket, the watch your

parent gave you if you would only mind

the hour. Months sink into the water and

the small rounded lump accumulates its

fair share of disuse. Dreadfully private,

pressed against the faces of circular

necessity, the pane gives way, transparent,

to a possibility of rectitude.

LIVE ACTS

Impossible outside you want always the other. A continual
recapitulation, & capture all that, against which our redaction
of sundry, promise, another person, fills all the
conversion of that into, which intersects a continual
revulsion of, against, concepts, encounter,
in which I hold you, a passion made of cups, amidst
frowns. Crayons of immaculate warmth ensnare our
somnambulance to this purpose alone.
The closer we look, the greater the distance from which
we look back. Essentially a hypnotic referral, like
I can't get with you on that, buzzes by real fast, shoots
up from some one or other aquafloral hideaway,
emerging into air. Or what we can't, the gentleman who
prefers a Soviet flag, floats, pigeoning the
answer which never owns what it's really about.
Gum sole shoes. The one that's there all the
time. An arbitrary policy, filled with noise, & yet
believable all the same. These projects alone contain
the person, binding up in an unlimited way what
otherwise goes unexpressed.

THE NEXT AVAILABLE PLACE

Out of luck, which repeatedly faces a catch, down
in the, else logic another dimension, legs upright,
collide, milk of the, eases the respecting,
plain bag, not rearrange not strange either, eminent bonnet,
articulated by half-jabs, reprehensible, reprehending,
triangular pulled out past shape, jog, collide,
reform, collide. Mindy, which sits on knocking, interest
in hard plants, layouts, the Nigerian Embassy comprehending
a Swiss observer Teamsters go to give, nod.
Like I lie here, unconvinced of the mood, tone,
half-light—half in bed, part removed. Like
I go out, stay still, leave alone, bend the round.
He sits foolishly and doesn't get any tickets.
Pattern a once remembered hope that one time. Seepage.
Alluvial fan belts of the delta. Incriminating
bus rides. Hold up, hold out. Narcissistic novel
reading, boat camping, sufficient entrance
space, lackluster discipling lawns at
stop in traffic, make sound that amaze,
prepositional annoyance, hits hat. At bat,
annoyance at resolve, replication, silly materials.
Withstand, remorse. Press buttons,
cots, make-shift haberdashery. With which they
rush all the time. Sermons and then earnest
proposals. Ether, Esther. Erstwhile. Largely
overoperated, insular. Balzac. Berkshire

hunting prospects. Holds you back, holds to you,
barely, bared by. Orthopsychiatry, opthalometrics,
gastrojejunerology, cryptopsychopathology,
oncogenetics. Molten circumferences crushed to
an order. Anyway, I don't hear the rest. That was why,
the voice, procuring, matter of digging, resistance
& desperate. Poland, Biebow. I mean mental
(physical). Without or else replaced. Dark or
dotted. Ill-set. Here's quite a sampling, hat check.
Furniture on rewind. Hind legs, top shape. Meteoric
fall of depression, algebraic happenstance.
Offbeat kind of velour. Beats a path straight
down here, falls on carpet, angles hopelessly.
Arch or else ineligible: scoff
tape, ineluctable warmth. Finish. Finesse.
Everywhere eels, intransigent. Floats down like items,
longed for air ineligible for memos about the time of
day, hardly perceived. Reptile, regrettable. Our
asked. Antithetic to team—*teems*
in my "head". Aloha, sit com, marmalada.
Urgent callings, beats brains, gets set. Relevant
roofing invalidates ochre oasis. A hand uh canasta.
Leadership, effectiveness under pressure, motivation,
decorum, easy living, schnapps, business cards,
the pretty little thing on the.... Memories
of residue. Average paraplegia. Parigi, Angleterre,
insouciance. That idea & half buckle buy you.

Curvacious slurs: misanthropy, cliquishness,
territoriality, misunderstanding. What is
described by the patient as 'dizziness'
has often not even the remotest relation to
vertigo. Labyrinthine irritation: sensation of
rocking, sensation of staggering, swimming sensation,
sensation of weakness, sensation of backward swaying,
wavy sensation. Which he wouldn't even begin to
talk about. We men as ourselves in flight, an
oblique response, & never coming up close to, stare
at, walls, hang gliders, Japanese shoe repair.
Iraqi, Iroquois. I felt stumbled, made the first
pretence, angled out. Unrealizable waltzes. Increment,
incarnate. An early riser but late to realize. "As if
this sleep...." Undigested, rubber ball. Incredible
pallor. Mercy minding me. All right: flamingos. Oblique
response: response. Or maybe it didn't even enter
into her mind. Flare. Float. Filtration.
Invisible only to himself (herself). Later,
I wondered if I had said the right thing, if
I looked okay. But it was only two o'clock—three
more hours still. Mind minimal. When sorrow left,
she left. Tugs, tug. Mrs. Happenstance had a happy
hysterectomy. Completely cold by now. Honest,
earnest. Poor insight, abnormal explanations,
suspiciousness, widespread remoteness, vague rapport,
preoccupation, irrelevance, restlessness. Pester,

Petrarch. Foreign body sensation. Misplaced modesty.
Like I like her. Lurker. Aimed well down. Issue,
is you. Framed then framed. Ill (I'll)
begets a. Unruly exstasis. Information to confound
bike past blue note harass (harness) looks to.
Imbibe, imbecile. Leeds' leading legend: IN FOR.
Nothing that I can say convinced me. With it, withheld.
Dread, scuzzy. Perhaps Polish (polish). I
feel rearranged, mandate a macaroon. Cuba,
Taiwan. Indubitable dauntress fraudulent at ever
attempting a view: binary, bisected, by the seaside,
beside myself. Relatively few. Instantly
benign. Bel canto. Silly trips to Everglades.
Invasive, extracurricular. Still, sill. Reluctant
energy. What makes a, of (small), gets, gathers,
alone it allures, my. Grossly premature. Defiant,
definite. Cut, cute. *Dignity robs us of our
dignity*. Grand Central Prism. On eaves of sand,
bearing us toward it. Rested, reliant. Malady
that knows no stop, hoarding its own devices, stretches
to trip, the raging confusion, obdurate, ironic,
metaled by temperance, exhaust

THE HAND GETS SCALD BUT THE HEART GROWS COLDER

As honor as mist arc that

           musing the fall

     & with this prompt

   shawls regret

              swath: the formation

       aims to qualms

 magnetic replicate

      certain amount of buzz

            is only what say

    murky entitles

       hammer alarm

intelligence of the

     closet in its hold

      odor of renouncing set aside

   lands of rolling distances

    mislaid before

       quiet submission

   drawers shut

            (floods, alight

        to grasp this

           exceptional alignment

     mirrored by

      accurate circuity

nowadays as we and

          such as when a person, secretly
         covering a wish to boast

characterize a although phase

              "special stage"

      impair its compelled

scattered, of, was

    heartily languid

               (the scarcity of premonitions

      adaptable

epic of steady—sensational—progress

         jelly, twine

   then up & just

      "complet monsieur"

        now this had gone to
        opposite extreme, which
        came as a surprise to
        us both, we
        gotten very quiet, mildly
        preoccupied with our
          extremely cautious and

      which, somehow, will devise

   (woke up

     the floor

  removed and

    dark pools with)

       repelled   riveted

   "I haven't so many chances left in this town"

part falling asleep, part contemporary

      swatch   echo

intelligent reassurance at no use

     "It's raining and an altogether unpleasant..."

is the weather   it always seems like

                         out of puff

        little obtrudes strikes to mind but has

on significant portion, just the
gradual, at the time, put, make,
& very, diving (without), which
'skater' has, minds what, look
just of, cloudy, absorbing,
watches, report

                so tired all my thoughts

frowns piercing with double flaw

      since what I had in vain I want
       & what in vain I sought I

   implies, other things being equal, will
      not hold, must so interpret,
          self-contradictory to suppose,

support intermingled with other

    partaken

        also status: link, harassment
           doing less: distribution,
                  mountains, strange:
            discuss, arch,

        RED

        PINK

        ORANGE

        PIMENTO

        LEMON

        ASH

        BLACK

        PURPLE

"I had never hit anyone intentionally before"

earned   gets glassed   boggles
innuendo curtain
rods   flagrant

implodes, implores

"all my body
wants to do is
look up my dress"

irreconcilably available

replay what it

delicacy crushes

So really not visit a remember to strange

A it's always finally seems now which ago

Long that by amazed guess I thing obvious of kind

Feel can weigh a has distance the off

That there it's then & you

While now which whatever point

Slipping constantly be to seems happening

Until fingers the like through sand

Staring there still on back look only can

Before yourself find the of window in thoughts your at

Combing again here & times a this over gone

That for inseam or beach of section

Peering the "yet &" where exactly or when sure longer

Results tangible of terms in is it as

Thought of splint a than more no all after is which hope

Somewhere catch to looking

Or ease the that here say can what

Preclude doesn't such of difficulty

In always of necessity harsher that

Circumstance different under place

Changed to seem yet &

Are by gone have that years if as

Real the if but record of matter a all

From reeling still were

Looking stop with begin to say to is which it

Puts us before to such

For necessity any rest

By if as tracings these of more

Of sort a well as

Is which place of kind one in stay to skill the with longer

Complete this view of point a than more

Annoys what here you're paper the

Unnecessary becomes flourishes

China in tea the all for again

As film the see to we are or

Else leap a such make to motivated be to need

Table this atop is solitary

Like issues discomfort of hang whatever

Mention to forgot I and you

Can't itself reform already

Like feel I want properly

The actually do to able will

Pressing more the feel to begin now

Rug the about to trips

Atumble time the by only night all window

Put that minute last the at panicking

An has delay the but expected than longer takes

On count that itself too much

Discerns imaginations a takes

I brim from handle look cluster from skyline

The same the much it find & side the over

STANDING TARGET

Deserted all sudden a all
Or gloves of notion, seriously
Foil sightings, polite society
Verge at just about characterized
Largely a base, cups and
And gets to business, hands
Like "hi", gnash, aluminum foil
Plummeting emphatically near earshot
Scopes bleak incontestably at point
Of incompetence, blasting back
Past imperceptible arrogance, islands of
Blown air, overlooked, replies
Startle, stares. Scans distance
(Arcane), his mittens in the
Other room: "Watch out for
That plane!" Heavy platelet
Material. A subdural transmissiveness
Asleep on the bus, as if, slowly
Trickles down the foreclosure, drifts
Through doors: lean, longed for. Threshold
Of choice at absolutely pushes, runways
Into bumping, obdurate, collapsing
In lapse, replacement minimal. So sad
Sitting there. Slows as sense
Descends, very oracular warmth
Would go by maybe years, unnerving.

Redress of slant. Limitless like
Listless. I aim at you, slips
Behind my back, that neither of us
Had told, kept.

"I've given you every break in the world."

The night arms itself against our invasion, a
Cyclic necessity that permits the ball
Of the heart's expectation. Restraint to
Give space to a line of conduct, feel
You there, trusting the mannerliness of
The sky's fullness, preempting
Aversion. The paths take you close
Rumors inhabit it, the lamps are
Dampened by quiet villainies, ashamed
To offend, quick to renounce. Ponderous
Steps awaken the ground to our
Ineptness, falling into the shaft
Stunned to be twenty floors below. The
Telephone rings, the mail box is empty
The coffee shops recede into layers
Of margarine and blank stares. Life itself
Inhibits its experience.

1. Throwing a tennis ball into the
air and clapping hands—up to four

times—before catching it again. 2.
Rolling a tennis ball underfoot in
a zig-zag pattern between six
matchboxes lined up a short distance
from each other (timed). 3. Threading
ten beads of 3 cm diameter (timed).
4. Inserting differently shaped
objects into appropriate slots (timed).

(saying:)
I am hungry, let me eat
I am thirsty, let me drink

How sad lines are, crisscrossing
out the hopes of an undifferentiated
experience, the cold sweeps
past, eyes tear, the night begins
again. I only hope you can
hear that, that its daze
returns the sting we lack.
Bellowing of our former
anticipation, gazing
backward, becoming conscious
of a future noticed only as
the rapid and continual receding
of a past.

All of a sudden all deserted.

Neurological impairment, speech delay, psychomotor difficulties with wide discrepencies and fluctuations, excessive neurotic fears and compulsive behavior, a diffuse hostile attitude, general clumsiness, confused dominance, poor fine motor coordination, asymmetrical reflexes, aggressive, callous, arrogant, excessive inhibitions, rebellious, suspicious, attention seeking, erratic friendship pattern, overexcitable in normal situations.

As President and Chief Executive Officer of Sea World, Inc., David DeMotte is responsible for managing all aspects of the Company's operations at Sea World parks in San Diego, Aurora, Ohio, Orlando, Florida, and the Florida Keys. A native Californian, DeMotte, and his wife Charlotte, enjoy hunting, fishing, and tennis in their spare time.

Hugh Chronister, President of Harvest Publishing Company, the Harvest Insurance Company, and the Harvest Life Insurance Company—publishers of five state farm magazines, several trade journals, and operators of a number of insurance agencies—is active in many publishing and agricultural organizations and a trustee of Baldwin-Wallace College, as well as being Director and President of the Ohio 4-H Foundation and a past president of the Audit Bureau of Circulation. Chronister, his wife, Marge, and their three children

live near Medina, Ohio. In his
free time his interests include
books, horses, golf, and Western
art.

Ralf D. Caulo, Deputy Director of the
HBJ School Department, arrived in New York
via Dallas. He spends much of his
time on the road, however, talking with
sales managers in all HBJ sales regions,
and visiting school districts and
school personnel around the country
to discuss trends in education, curricular
changes, and new programs. When
not involved with his job, Caulo enjoys
sporting events, and keeps in shape
by playing tennis and racket ball. He
also maintains an interest in history,
especially American history, and is
currently focussing on the period of
industrial expansion between the 1870's
and 1900.

The end result was a gradual

neurosis superimposed upon a pre-existing

borderline character structure.

Note the exclusive right-side-up feature.

Awkward constellation

points, margins

washed "in good

voice", vanished

in good voice. Delirium

tyrannizes the

approximate moment.

To vanish

outside

the circuit.

If anyone has blossomed this season
Charlie has! On arrival at camp he was
reserved, really a watcher. He slowly
and carefully entered our routines. Once
we were alerted to his misgivings at
having been absent we planned several
jobs for him in the room, sent him on errands
all over camp, discussed absences in a
general way. He was very relieved to discover
that many of his group had been
in the same predicament; this seemed
to ease his concern. Since this time he
has become much more relaxed in general, laughs,
gets into boy mischief, really
acts at home here. Much
of the time he is a pretty serious
fellow, but more and more we see Charlie
forgetting his mien and living the
life of a pretty frisky little boy.

Charles has done extremely well in swimming.
Throughout the season he
gave close attention to instructions and
conscientiously practiced quietly on
his own during part of "free swim" before
going to fun with the other boys and
pool assistants. He had only one difficulty—
one foot persistently
stuck to the floor of the pool. Last
week Charlie got that foot off the bottom

and swam completely across the
pool. The beam
on his face was a pleasure to see! But
he was much to shy to talk about it,
of course.

Last spring Charles put himself on record
that he didn't like crafts. We soon
came to understand his feelings
when we worked with him. Charlie
is not strong in manual dexterity. (This
may be part of a mixed dominance
situation Mrs. B. and I discussed in
relation to tying shoes.) Fortunately,
what he lacks in developed skills
he makes up for in
patience, determination, and
knowledge of what he wants as
results.

Charlie has grown to enjoy our organized games
His interest carries throughout the
period, as a rule. He pulls his share in
team set ups and cheers loudly for
his team. During free time Charlie
has succeeded in busying himself with
friends. Sometimes it's Running
Bases, or digging for coal, or
club meetings in the
"private hideout".

     fatigue

        of   of

       open for

    to   , sees

doubles

glass must

  are for

in : they

    , her

  that it

watches, leaves,

    days that

  made

and the

    The

     to plates

  all shaped

    am

must get

  it if not

  or

houses, beginnings

newly

   hind an

  other here

    Give

come to

off,

   an

Fluency in gain has remedial comprehension
The Course of improvement shown again, noticeably

Benefiting errors, numbers, a more certain

Knowledge to vary need, type of work,

Continuous manner of representing alertness,

Game of ball, confused when dictation, outgoing

And generally broadened social adjustment at

Personal endeavors, which is not always

Available, in and fundamentals in,

Silent reading and oral spelling,

Discussions, fair play, group life—

Pattern of careless work and sloppy

Appearance—included is integral,

Quiet and rather vague, at one period,

Skills and coordination, enthusiastic business,

When in actuality the class had merely,

And often both. He seems to feel depressed

And unsure of himself. I hoped,

Holds himself back by doing, this is

Especially true, omits many times.

FOR LOVE HAS SUCH A SPIRIT THAT IF IT IS PORTRAYED IT DIES

Mass of van contemplation to intercede crush of
plaster. Lots of loom: "smoke out", merely
complicated by the first time something and don't.
Long last, occurrence of bell, altitude, attitude of.
The first, at this moment, aimless, *aims*. To the
point of inordinate asphalt—lecture, entail.
These hoops regard me suspiciously. A ring
for the shoulder (heave, sigh...). Broadminded in
declamation, an arduous task of winking
(willing). Weary the way the world wearies,
circa 1962. The more adjoins, sparklet and parquet
reflection, burned out (up). Regard the willing,
whose movement be only remonstration, ails
this blue bound boat. The numberical tears.
Edged out where tunnels reconnect, just below
the track. Aims departing after one another
& you just steps away, listening,
listless. Alright, always—riches
of that uncomplicated promise. Who— what—.
That this reassurance (announcement)
& terribly prompted—almost,
although. Although censorious and even more
careless. Lyrical mysticism—harbor, departing
windows. For love I would—deft equator.
Nonchalant attribution of all the, & filled with

such, meddles with & steals my constancy, sharpening

desire for that, in passing, there, be favorite

in ordinary, but no sooner thought than gone. My

heart seems wax, that like tapers burns at light.

Fabulous ephemera a constant force for giddy flight.

But boxes both in, boated just the same. Mass of fix,

the further theorizing a final surrender, until the next, thins

or becomes transported, nights asleep, day wondering.

Appearance that not so much won't shake but returns, as

the pilot turns his starship into wool. To knit

these phantasmagorias out of white, sheer monument to culture's

merry meal of itself. In eyes that look with mirror's blankness,

remoteness complete—I want but all recedes. Motor

fixation, streetcar trace, the last days of this

water, these fields. To sustain such blows and

undermine the lash is memory's cure. At long

last, image reconciled to friend, chatting

under oaks, rays of a sky no longer our

but all the more possessed. For much that has

no cure. Duplication equal to charm of happier times, those that

disappeared, faster and more fantastic, the loud

despair the softer homily. A shoe entails

its path till, foot on foot, no diversion's

seen. The sky parts, the blinds repair.

A hush that skirts the subtler moment,

the cumbersome charade of weekend and reply.

This darkness, how richer than a moat it lies. And

my love, who takes my hand, now, to watch all this
pass by, has only care, she and I. We deceive
ourselves in this matter because we are in
the habit of thinking the leaves will fall or
that there are few ways of breaking the circuit.
How much the stronger we would have been had
not—but it is something when one is lonely
and miserable to imagine history on your side. On
the stoop, by the door ledge, we stand here, coffee
in hand. Roll top desk, undisguised goodbyes. I
wait but I don't want it. Austerely premature,
scrutinized to the point of a gazeless graph, no past
there, how could it hope to mean to us. These
are the saccharine days, the noiseless
chirps of the sublimated depths. By the train
tracks, halfway down, sitting there, looking at—
a goat knows no better sound. What of colors, what
of characters—anoint with all precision
projection brings, so much sturdier and
valorous than ourselves. Depressed eyes
clutter the morning and we drown in a sea of
helping hands. Better the hermit than the sociopath.
Destruction? —the wind blows anyway, any where,
and the window frame adorns the spectacle. That
person fixes in your head, and all the world
consumed through it.

SIMPLE PLEASURES

Consolation of way by not is understandable

Bogus monotony the far in which territory

Limited a only gives global map the on

Line red a like political ignored the by

Water, territory we and rocks that such

Subjects are from and ourselves force of it

Parts exclude finally becomes products, capsule

Escape more contained a place, extension

Massive the because us persuading for account

Complete on rely which of some complicates

Withstand accredited the traduce our Moscow

Will prevent stains no longer, a needs

Future, expropriation an of subject the and

Recognized might parade whose expectation

Think ground to have or do in time

And into enter, known without passes

Not if I even of depth, eyes

As more anything is, are, axis grouped by told

Almost chronology evident to say approach sliding

Whose hiding be only bare conscience

What of delight renounce, choose

Neither you or myself, profit what

It makes to sound, aloud in my

Charity, believing all things, himself

Wakeful, sought profit that of seen

Grieve faster for faults, together

According upon supply what began
Point therefore ease, offending
Intimidation of means, consist in
Representing as something invariable
Removing without killing, as soon that
Strength, visible into certain kinds
Work at earnestly forming monuments of
Pathos, service encouraged by spectacles
Infancy of place, yet in whose dishes
Hungered itself wholly, troubled which
Awaits all that is needed, occupations
Merely flourishes design that renounce all
Mystified allotments, accurate to calibrate
Salubrious enchantment, missions in weigh
Of which recoil at settings, surround
Large cement bystanders, irksome commands
Regarded—hurled—when this is
Carried above, and roars, "By these..."
So necessity persuades which acquired
Eloquence equates—lashes with exposition
Laps upon the stage, insights
Without peril recalled adequate to majesty
Most powerful, not held in result
Damaged all by feeling same loss
Interred at passion to cross wisdom
Neither tanned nor trimmed by
Blanks at stare or passion

Encircles calm denoting skew in commands

Move to hand the mind at once turn

By fall is slate, evanescence

Cope in utmost luck this awkward

Ground saw to make refinements succeed

Pastels to bestow an example pampered again

Myself of fool prevailed in short

Ambition increased given by low

Opinion still more compact to told

Part sums give pace to quell

Little by asking, hope misplaced

Best sought at pasture's fashion

Renounce this by itself did gnaw

Tide of swell or not in gain

Suffice—I too this breath an air

More nightly seen, quench and put

Off what hands by haste impell

Shortly to quake and call

Else air frightful cause because sums

Part at aging, faction regrets by

Daily chord returns to fend

Goes damp with hoop replies, disposing

Marbled doting stand on rote

Repairs what habit's done accedes

For chance, routine, displayed or rave with

Themselves equal, operate to order in

Censoring empty fact, value

Which polity withstands, ashamed, what victors
Erase, forgotten first forgetting—stylize
Holds only one's solitude's mistrust, recovery
Simpler, nothing provoke what has at
Any interfere, happening, shouts like those
To want I do, but changed because
We live it's those describe, who turn
Showing what winds the tip, visible
Dimensions' outer flight, infers in what we
Clad, day since the more its much
Become completely attachments, similarity
Toward one protected, else stop to
Sleep, towards altitude, simply leading
Beyond what we've become—mistaken
Drafts of inarticulated wants
Haphazard against the banners of
Remorse, writ large from hope, downcast and
Reassembled, assembling, to which the heart
Grows closer still—to hear all this at
Time, the smug and listless waits upon
While you—

THE BLUE DIVIDE

An almost entire, eerie, silence floats above and between the fixtures that separate me from the doorstop. Slight rattle, rolling, scratches the space just behind me, which is helpful, if not necessary, to cast the reflections and echoes in just the way I'm accustomed. A table and window frame sit just ahead, to the side of the walls and corners, slat wood flooring, shelves, the tar-blacked driveway and terraced approach roads. A person waits in a boat about an hour away, floating in totally occasional manner. Stripped of its wood, unparalleled in respect to its riveting and displaced glare, incised by its dimensions, I feel the slight pang of an earlier sensation which rapidly switches in succession to images harder to identify at first, postcard sized shapes, rolling vertices. The sounds are pervasive and only from time to time increase in loudness which looks almost as if it were a tear or rip in the otherwise unbroken intensity. Bits of fabric—plaid, striped, glyphic—hang from fan gliders about 20 feet above and to the side arced formations of smoke languidly drift this way and that. Several hours pass the mood indiscernibly shifting to less substantive pleasures, the hallway rotating airily to the tempo of unforeseen reverberations. A small coterie remains behind to see that the ship departs smoothly, counting their change with an alternating frenzy and tedium. You ask for the lighter but remain seated, seem to recollect what you refused to say, purse your lips and, with a forlorn look, lapse back into thought, then begin to make suggestions for lunch. A fly makes its path spiralling over the campsite, arching toward the partially lit skylight and barraging full throttle into the screen. Men in blue suits and brown hats hurry over to the table and unpack their cases, gesticulating animatedly with their feet and hands.

A tall, thin boy with grey callow eyes stares across the walk with forced attention, rubbing his legs and scratching his head, finally sinking into a dull, dejected slump which nonetheless gives the impression of greater ease. Barrels of fruit, uncovered and ageing, fill the area with a distracting odor, the inevitable subject of recurring fantasies for civic improvement. Tendrils, assimilated into the background glare, announce with glum resignation "far better for those with lighter hearts" imminent departure. Blocked, buoyed, incessant, I take for the elevator, dash quickly to the folded bed clothing—you angling loosely toward the courtyard, suffused with contentiousness. After a long walk we return to an almost identical place—the mat on the one side, the hobby horse on another. Paralyzed by the smoke, dazed by the duplicity, an earnest but elderly gentleman hobbles somewhere along the periphery, stooping, circling, tumbling, gliding while making his way to an adjacent watering hole. Not so nimble or quick-witted, the pool attendants make a final resolution to shore up their energies and make a clean break of it. By now the helicopter is annoyingly late and a considerable queue is backed up to the presenting section, obtrusively disrupting the ordinary course of commerce. I get on the megaphone and make these several points but the indifference turning to scorn of the onlookers is too uncomfortable and I turn to a medley of disconnected hits. You look so quiet there it seems a shame to disturb you, eyes lolling about to their own tune of distraction. The icy slope curves beyond reach, careless of index and anticipation.

FOOTLIGHT PARADE

We meet as we our files

Fills empty air is

Detachments as of what

Else having said, say

What beats untidily

Moderate inclination, loquacity

Stooped, compelling misapprehension

Incomplete to drift, inside

All case, buttons for behavior

Furnishing outline the like of which inquire

Idea with reach in nobody

Have to wonder of

A shift brought, unseats

A cleaner building face, wave

As signal become warp, plank

To tussle, assigned in wager's digest

Crankily skip, worry for worse

Whatsoever docks the levelling

Select assail or cartwheel, boycotts

Terrific terror sums equal

Counting about lobes, furnished

Films for whatever might be noticed

Might unnerve, as easily

Burn out or through, overlook

Within us brought to house of

Sight, that enter and divert

Knocking by occupant's congestion
Strewn of sheaf

WARD OF THE WORLDS

From outside, about eight feet, the bell marchers mark a conspicuous trail back to the agent's landing. Small palpitations announce an unseen presence, hidden below the line of the shore, more lethargic than the women in uniform who defy gravitational pull with sanguine resignation. Boats arrive at intervals filled by the frames through which they bounce, battalions of inaccuracy lining the crevices with immediate recognition. Not tubular really green chairs, white lattices, checkered floors with manifesting histories, blotter the same dressing area, stages in convex incapacity, electronic in feel, spiked, architectonic.

A hand, aroused by the same incoherent projection, repeats protectively the motions of semblance, wind or shale. Basic malice, flap or intention, momentum of remonstrance, an awareness too strained, & back to the barking insignia. Republic of drain, alone by the pump, the bars by the sea, shelves of indifference coated with flairs.

Dip premised on glare. A hobbling demeanor taken for ethics & straightaway the resounding clip, note on the door, who staring, boards in bed, portrays the outside chance.

Step of a locus, amorized on sunken, glisten, hardly. Caution to casement, standards to pall.

Breakfront in headway to green carpet, long table, set up to pry with formica fluting, around the criterion, dashing and doting. Become telephoned, originally oxymoronic and stultifyingly pleasant. A nice coat and tea chain, too bad for the hat. Grateful for melon and minutely characterized, the green grocer throws a ball at the film usher. Rumpled and hideous, compiled out of promise, all gushy and surprised to be used to the complexion. A triumph of headlights.

Obviously intimately, the duration at pains to remove, showing that he would leave beats & somewhere. A function fit into something I've missed, but then maybe you're hitting on the smaller (pictures inside to) pertain, garage, contrasting there's got stems on specific tidal pull, or by cutting (counting) anticipate projects underneath.

Reduced to decry tables of topics, minions mercurially decked out, notorious current to the practice of dead meter. Through the rich perceptions of the hour the stomach gets all cramped & dodges the Central Spirit. That seems related to your point but not worth perusing.

Placate to induce what rails the lining. Here the insolence of name, in the way of terrific armatures. Go plaster the arena and brandish the pylons, reregarded now as all too popular, though in no time shakes a bit lank. Spun of drift, quelled of bone.

Bending which breaks against the floor's reason, chance that fails by succeeding pulls—the raving enclosures and articulate clumps. Spoken in the off-white, part perplexed arcade, a span of feet turned to hours. Taking this mist as bolt or outline, emphatic slinking to denote militant flags in seceding equations.

The wages of Protestant taxicabs.

A determinist ethic holds sway as the great masses of the people wait to be interviewed. References don't check out. Heads involve hobbles. The employable count up on the hands of one finger. The elegant outlet, all plugged up nice—their own reward for mascara. A coat, to coast, glittering entombment to the last. These white chests perspire with fading industry.

It took about two weeks but never mind about the postage. Slight rolling, maybe garbled concern—you could just about learn to record the torsion. Precision with which to reactivate old mannerism, tick, notice, dry mouth. Cooperate to stairwell. Great monumentality—all fluffed up, shouldered, red dress. I browse accordingly. Flush monsters. Leftover lecture. Pressure abides by accordingly. Mosaic strip, apropos the.

Seeing pink curtain entail what pinker. Shop window relates moment's rest, eye to floor. Estimate level of demi-urge, sunken feeling, wake all night by counting, makes review come in order to gulp potholes—what they want being adamant, recessed. Brooks no truck. Arm's length—shoo in.

The light fell: the woman with the sheepish smile rivets the upholstery. I get all shook up and head for the fire exit but trip on the celluloid transparency all bundled up in the middle of the aisle. One even two features go by, the trailers are repeated, a person with a bubbling button hole reaches for the pantry. Escalators of innocence annihilate the track. An overstuffed blue box reveals the seven types of misunderstanding, a lecture likely to make the tired morbid and the alert psychotic. The boat is docked at the window, the radio blasts at 30 second intervals: Go Away. Far off, the inlanders are estimating husk sizes, sorting through the swatches to identify the weave.

Destination occurs at every stop & to glide through, oblivious of the darker resemblances, is to rejoin in that charade that occupies dead space. The coffee burned, the occasion determines, as, meeting in the hall, stooped in the shuttle, holding on the receiver. Prints are emblems of larger things than we, the housing for the bulb is still in English.

Premonition sags, the maps of the hats take flight, drawers and glasses are emptied. Shapes, only without form or color, tumble through the bush. Staplers, humidors, boots paper the parkway, imbued with maxims—the heave and heather of a complacent visit.

A sigh employs a glance—cabinets to bolster all impressions, hearts akimbo. Crack hits beach, boy sands barometer. Nefarious misdeeds, hardly amounting to more than a misshuffled deck, studiously pose, loosely rebuke. I spot a pretzel vendor and detain him outside the luggage rack. Down a blintz, go another block. Two seats by the blinking camera.

Pushcarts pass along the untended hour: forever to declaim far announcements. A tap at the door—sock or blouse repair what stream of sharpened fazing. The great fear in the identification with, how, for instance, stand up and say, run for. Own importances regard floor for hammer—suture with confirmed dissuasion. Repugnance to cool cafeteria—here what ails by aiding middrift. Oppose what bends in gauge: frankly stippled, emboss.

Robins indolent as trays.

Sundry, the sardonic chug on the elusive bridge, crested, perhaps pounce, vacantly to infer what mitigates sounder aim. The oracular walk, judgments that pass at clip untenable to tone, tear of harsher modulations. Inattentive warmth, a smoke in the bush, unfended.

Coats of candescence land approximate to the holding pattern. Pizza fizzes to the ragged polyrhythms of the Macombo beat. Black shoes, then green, pole-vault to the lead in all-Anglican competition. Replacement valves upend the tiled toilet seats. The subway hurtles its passengers to a periphery just outside the range of the reach of the jostled jet setters back from a week in Lumbago. The fat go by way of the third rail, a.k.a. fifth force or second column.

Obviously I'm absorbed. I was so caught by; tracking; materiality; remarkable amount of practically enormous static; catch on; "priorities" as; dole, an interesting. Boulevard Stucco. Which eyes upend. Shuttle bunny. Nuance Garage. Close Encounters of the Apoplectic Kind. Macy's, Bamburger's, butter pecan, chartreuse, Idlewild. World the over all & home: legtimate to the. Observations, much to to central as I'll also; again; totally of/out, splits its; to, for, was, which, "confluence'', i.e. like to the; might like; package; noting; extend.

Sail to note obtrusion jointly. Fazist mannerisms at/or Louis Quatorze impishness. Aplomb makes beeline answer to pertain. Lourdes-a-leaping: phonograph distension. Here the romance, albeit *in camera*, sustains the chaste chiaroscuro of the lumbar regions. Don't fret up the walkway, belittle the sanitary apologies. She provides lessons in identical—frozen trip-ups—fundamental to obtain mixed blessing. He harpsichords the ghost.

Latinate heirs prepare the boy for pears. Mosaic memoranda placate subtle tutlege. The eyes of Kitty O'Donoghue stare down the long, thin aquamarine corridor.

Saturation amounts variously to portions unintended for caliber. Activity hails to delinquent feint, supper for arrested dearth, pins the bluish diligence. Articles of favor obliterate the fox terriers. Today, the seered *vox humana* profits only to be lard for Sunday's breakfast. Plead, please. Park the parole pester the poltergeist. Pump the spittoons.

A lack memorizes a tune, cheap ditty to infect cerebral recess. Pulse of dissension, order of enervate. Sometimes silken sometime airless, mops of tops shriek artless disclaimers. You in the pale coat, you in the out-moded housegoods store, you craning your head a full yet meager measure. All these things written, served up.

Enunciation of nautical brackets, castanets of the eloped criterion.

Assumption of alarm. From ordinary tendency make sputter on regard the like of makeshift. Infer fast shakers, close the falling window. Goads line, wrinkle cushion, votes for periodic drift of the continental shelves.

Evanescence, some complain, and what other matter of deportment do you bother to adjourn so abruptly. The wind, sunstroke, tuna casserole: an appointed case. She slips on tunes of sand, mazing in her way the vocable tangents of doctored assent. The blooms, the dips and spans....

The stones are astonished—they make their waves simper through the embankment, pausing to curve at the precise indictment, shattering totally. Homily for the loftily born, who now sing at angles approximate to dark climates. Raise the foil, curl the needle! Reverence mounts the podium, odorizes hall air.

PUTS WHATS ARGUES

Stares can be immediately
expressed. Highway crater
alerted to waterbound alarm.
Hence what feelings test. Month
of sundries. Mind from which
window entrap, sail of aluminum
batter, what then farmed in
nylon oblique. Seeming rest, seeming
silly. Shock of which rebound
dilates. Motion of bracelets, brackets
weigh along four-poster, nocturnal in
descent, sets upon. For instance,
jewel when you mean pawn. A
pushed and wrinkled reputation
closing in on private sector.
Notion of pane, of wrap—hear
otherwise guards in other room.
Farmland stretched as stretch may—copious
tabletop, blank ceiling (forecast). Intransigence,
persistence—steps of of self forged
(sloped) coupons. Reruns to disk.
Faced of aversion clips to. Clips
to frequency join. So fellow rotates
amble of business—permission
of alibi roads some appointment.
Various of so, itself of part

all at with get, could I only the
was there in piece any or these of one.
On focus seemingly effaced. Tendencies
of parameter into locked that
in fact assume comprehension. Something
together taken, pointed at remark.
So that so so an inkling forfeit
reminder. Here he's shake. People
out there loop throwing really at
limp. Appreciate your taking,
you raise too indeed would
posture in charting, able to
since we being just has perhaps
found—ends, curiously—all too
action alone. Realm into often
or dismissed, would I & as
operating, encompassing, am if.
Paralysis or the to contribute.
Invisible explicitly or umbrella
manner. Political sufficiently
or political evidently. Crucial
on touch, as it itself cannot
touch. Instigates you to—context
falls into the—but your letter ends.
I actually have no real
disagreement, do not particularly
feel at odds with what. Else

anything, that all, compared
to, that nothing should.
& meaning not to, to
do whatsoever says, does. Why should
love be constructed so, restricted
so. By channels, then take to
channels. Always a certain trade
off that ends up being paid
for. Aside like seem can this, that's,
you do. But just
criticize and aggrandize?—inaudible.
Invisible in the
way our bodies get in the way
of, and yet only by, only through.
Is is that but is the is
its also mysterious backlighting.
Place into fall, being brought into,
held, something like sounded,
flustering over my. Specific
forms suggesting. Until very recently
the idea that he or you, so really in
general, & this is partly true, ie
can see confluence, & mistake all that,
or not see, skid, institutionalizing
faults, double play, honest to
you & honest, trying to isolate.
Covered, already covered. But then perhaps,

68

yet the reason I, in this sense,
cataloguing characterizations. Of
position in put, these getting of, as
exactly but, intent of part up
ends is just as thing such
talk to sense, thinking into easily
fall. If I speed up at this
point response degenerates. Disappearing
except what just. Relatively mundane &.
Undiscriminately almost all possible levelling.
Sensorium abound question the regard,
flotilla, left of smoldering. Piled
afternoons to mind and fence. Whiplash.
Stadium restores—demure foment. By
double cross removes the ample
corner, retreat to, suspended
last at flight, interior dislocation
foment on object, settles. Prosthetic
brain magnetizes hysterical boundaries
fundamental actions designate. Trust
what's. In that case,
I think it's, at the sheer, much
less, go about, since you ask, actually
tears in his, isn't it enough that,
now I'm merely, may
as well. Fortune will attest to to
spaced-out gymnastics. The soft focus

of having said anything at all, words
come to meditate a moment. Continual
coming back to dissolving into
totally directive slump as
ego promises fanbelt. I spy and
along comes mood pleat. So social
dynamics relax onto lily pads. A
sudden and impartial approach—
not on his feet more than eight
minutes and it's buzz time. Or:
get ready for the blitz parade.
Ideas of order at Fort Lauderdale,
Belmore Hotel, Sanchez Room. Very
alarming disconnection and or
realignment. The beauty of the
bus—all elongated, tires upfront, no
repercussions. Don't try that
Aristotle stuff on me. "She measured
to the hour its solitude." End of day,
head rains on shoulder. I bump
myself on low dive, certainly
silly to alarm arrangements
any more than clarify. These
beef have got stem, stamina.
Pencil fixes option up at fifth
floor. Maids marvel no frypan
empties joint seat. Get approach,

sends amulets. Front these buttons.
Awake as having had, what for once
with all to lose, yet her, in seeing,
frosts my patience. Duplicity
avow what cornered edges strike,
mends flight in falling,
breath decant. One body
but two hearts, stung at fortune's
height. Otherwise better get these
tracks out of here. Pajama rewind
on sofabed. Tertiary ties. Becomes
off the beat condominium, fellow
travellers of the foaming particulars. Damaged
by response, clubs down battered monuments,
burlesque of thought's refrain. I get in
way of solemn sequence, believe in torn
goods. Issues uncommonly commingle, heart
flaps, hands spurts. My such lurking
fantasies, cerebral honeycombs crest,
white walls rebuke. Agency unbend, resolve,
return to flow. Lipstick of the
granular archangel, slips soaking up
continental high-life, fortnightly,
as rain turns to shoulderblades.

ISLAND LIFE

Except that we sail and quit the horizon. Desperate
or even remotely concerned, waves between
and the air a constant source of
the old jangle, musters for itself new conduits
restless maybe for the things we never use, a half
haze, half shadow, modestly a project of
absorption in time, cast about, contentment
its own course. Persons who, parsimonious
of number, as just prospers final notice:
force native of finish—hold, take, what
by legion endure, a sturdy armor of fiction
facts the oasis gleaned from time and
pruned to witness vast resources, a hollow
measure, indeed, to fight this voracity of
pleasure's gleam, solid matter
brief digest for the Eternal's enfolding. We
meet again on such a field and I hand
you the shadow in my keeping, a blackish
truss surrounded by aisles of penultimate
surface. The swarm: that by victory retails
its angularity, impressing with silhouetted
display, by brink an eerie conjuring
of a still frame, luminous, transparent, edged to
submission. At once the signal is given—
it is as though one sudden mad impulse
simultaneously flings open every
gate, the throng issuing—

pouring—forth in a vibrating
stream that melts into space: a
double or triple dissolution, incalculable and
uninterrupted, cascading to an ultimate height
of 100 feet before returning to ground. One
night, hiding in my tree, I suddenly see a
man appear. Here place out of habit
subordinating to accidents of origin that so
often cause chance to loose
in things all of whom observe. The
gathering, hunched into statues, and
though be a guide, weathers into apraxia—
it's now, what, almost five weeks: and so
the network of realities that was the state, &c.
Knotted, inardent, mouthpiece of give and try.
Like you saying this thing you're too
wrought up or I never could get into
that, felt put out by the tension. Other:
its from, form, destruction outside, bent
something of viewed, challenge to what
supplanting, finally, eclipsing, out as shutting
unheard (unseen) the alongside. Natives
by replaced being natives present actually
to allow that, a society create to aim for the.
We are now, let's you by, pales in competition
to. & I had always imagined the thing, even
of a fourth, finished, even so defined, in

addition—& I'm convinced that— we've
never: talking small, throw up our hands, used
to fill & I feel a kind of clarity
if anyone else, numbers but as you
yourself, that "out there", & what I, also
would, it's like missing the first (pessimism
& discouragement discarded as) bravado, exclusionary &
certainly understood much better, I'm sure
I cast a real physical &, but, although
especially, as, as I was thinking, have
different advantages, in a somewhat
negative way, activity are appreciated &
taken with typical—"what did you expect"—for
hangers on or, & do people a really
amazing, pursuits, gets, quite legitimate.
My own interest is scale, filled with disavowels.
Is out to diffuse, is that you tap, than repeating
within is to begin to want, which would
be, it is this look of (whatever that) instead
of (which would be), anyway, we're, and in
that time would like, if that's, which
then leads you to see, maybe suggest
excursions, so to understand
the relations as inexorably linked, wholly
on edge, as dazzling as
its coy flipness and once
admirable. Just miles with scarcely a care (the

most jungle-like and impart) on these—
since we're spending, every once and a
great simultaneous. Which I keep
thinking back on in this soon to
become, based on, I can get for that, difficult
and as those set up, less a somehow but.
Squashed at bottom, thing in the since.
You could equally well choose Normandy French, Peasant
Yellow, Farmhouse Italian, or Primitive Colonial. This
has endured very much and I have parted or
partly willing (featherweight, Lindenhurst), ministering
to the outraged and diffident adherents to bygone....
At the other extreme, it
has not been my intention to say much about
curtains. *Una camera doppio, por favor.* The only
lensless camera our own heart (mind). Behind
every plate a promise, but events don't
alter circumstance. Ministries
of uncertainty, the bloodless click of the chapel's
eschatological memoir. Yet, for the
good no reform is possible, for the wicked none
conceivable—and so the world drifts
into stasis, imagining propriety, living out—
For some time I felt this way myself, it was
not until my eleventh year that the axial
geometry of morality took headway in my
thinking. Anecdotal gloss, immeasurable filing out.

The same tree that I looked out on yesterday
constantly shifting and changing in the light, here
a different leaf, there an unnoticed shadow, so that
it unrolls its story at every moment, fills
all eyes. These constants: of blue, a light touch
of pianoforte vaguely receding, of dulled green.
Hopping to the corner, insisting to the ladder.
A vague touch of constantly shifting. Her eyes
on. Most resplendent, hand in pocket, coat
tucked in. Beside illuminated hard rolls I
hardly care a jot. Jelly doughnuts, singular
suits, the faded salute. Time only but
for change, make its character, see
others there, lives, on caravans of speculation. An
omnibus of unsupportable clamor invested in the
prior—how mercurial, how agile, how. Absolutely
no clouds—only a few—and the
locust have.... I don't
ask for yellow, a sailor robe, magic boxer
shorts. Pole vaulting into clouds of odious
humor, second thoughts, mulled over, make
believe. Haze or mist or "honor his voice in". Honor
that dwells in cliffs, aside moments, location locked.
Forensic bouts with the subterranean, the quotidian
displacements, marshal the limp and enervated customs
of disquieted patrimony. "You have painted this picture
for me but you have misconceived my desires

76

taste and direction." Bellow, bore, benumbed
borealis. Basically a swift kick, the pick
up, the pantomine. No more feeling than an
imagined waistcoat. But as to machines, its own brightly
lit and frowns no more, the gentle rhapsody of
the marginal, the frightened hollyhocks and
grazing furrows, each to portray a
version of that timeless time, shadow
without shadow, that our nostalgia
clings to and our reason discounts.
When, in the darkness over me, issue of
its own substance, no calm, no rest
and all abuzz together, such
as when (the measure of the wise and
strange) I hear your voice
call, furl, blue-gloss, silken—
and the thick white bells....
It is this magnificent trumpet note
of the "crowded hour" that thrills
through even the most run-me-down occupations, exchanging
cordial sentiments with all, "as if they were
blood relations". For the aim was to create
a society that could be nothing but: native, terms
allow, in place, erase. And so the, which forces
in the usual manner (nameplate, curate, &c). Harshly
absorbent, lamplight, and the dark, impenetrable roads. By
held may be a shelving into the deepening sea, or

by any other frame a flit, funicular, flotsam.
A monument to the laconic majesty
of the cherished thought, the neglected hope, the
belabored insurrection. Of all these infested
and recalcitrant follies, I go with
the blue one, now again green, triangulated.
So much for the road show of unsupportable
stupor, the lockets of urgent
visitation—Urbino, Padua, Lausanne. Weighing
in at, crossing breeds with. The Mayor
has closed all bridges—even odd even
odd—and brunches, as the strike at the fading
fortifications continues (let me in, I'm going to feed
the zebra, loosen the windowpane). The excess of
calcification in no way diminishing the lack
of pretension to historical importance made
all the more grotesque by the increasingly fluid
remonstrations they made toward each other.
But this not to impede the respect each one had
for the other and for the land they loved. What
made the deepest and most longlasting impression, the
ballasts hoisted, the flute music mercifully shut
off, the students happily hidden from the unnerving
stare of the spinsterish Secretary of Commerce
as he trudges to the murky lagoon just by the neo-classical
library, the scattered rocks making the
otherwise sandy beach troubling to stroll on.

I had faced many problems before, felt your
silence a disturbing but temporary situation, hoped
you would understand and not entirely
be annoyed at me. Three o'clock
four o'clock—counting minute by minute. Molar
responsibility a new lollipop for the toads who
inhabit the public parks. Not
one minute, not to be diminished. Glaze
of last sunlight steeplechasing within
out of this world slaphappiness. A balloon
for the shoulders, lifting the spirits to instructive
levels. We jot down notes and move to the next
square, embankment, meeting ground, template. How
much happier than he who returns to the walks
already walked, the dinner already eaten, the
reflection already cast. "Well, souls never touch
their object." Heightened, extended, deeper—dimensions
for a platoon of hippies on holiday, much the
more admirable than we who sit here all agaze
at the dull plaid exteriors of the universe's
cores. Bumbling and amorous, hesitation the fixed idea
of desire's design. Hearing the way the world
hears—mystified, assuredly. Three mail boxes
starkly outlined against a pasture, the covered
sporting car, a dented bluejean, an uprooted
illegible flag. Need that blankets what
parsimony refrains—canopies of the refugee.

79